I KNEW TWO METIS WOMEN

The Lives of
Dorothy Scofield and Georgina Houle Young

Gregory Scofield

POLESTAR
BOOK PUBLISHERS

Polestar Book Publishers acknowledges the ongoing financial support
of The Canada Council; the British Columbia Ministry of Small
Business, Tourism and Culture through the BC Arts Council; and the
Government of Canada through the Book Publishing Industry
Development Program.

Cover design by Val Speidel.
Photo of the Metis sash by Brenda Hemsing.
Author photo by Blaise Enright-Peterson and Barry Peterson.
Cover and interior photos from the author's collection.
Printed and bound in Canada.

CANADIAN CATALOGUING IN PUBLICATION DATA
          Scofield, Gregory A., 1966-
          I knew two Metis women
          ISBN 1-896095-96-8
          I. Metis women — Poetry. I. Title.
          PS8587.C61412 1999   C811'.54   C99-910218-4
          PR9199.3.S29712 1999

LIBRARY OF CONGRESS CATALOGUE NUMBER: 99-61828

POLESTAR BOOK PUBLISHERS
P.O. Box 5238, Station B
Victoria, British Columbia
Canada   V8R 6N4
http://mypage.direct.ca/p/polestar/

5 4 3 2 1   Canadä

For those two most incredible women.
And for Aunty Donna, Aunty Shirley, Mom Maria,
Michelle, Virgie and the generations to come.

I KNEW TWO METIS WOMEN

EARLY COUNTRY FAVOURITES

HONKY TONKIN'

HOME ON THE RANGE

Love and thanks to Michelle Benjamin, my friend, sister and publisher whose continued support and belief in my work means more to me than words can express; Lynn Henry, my gracious editor, with whom it has been a great privilege to work; and Emiko Morita, whose good sense and publicity management have been instrumental to my writing career.

Love and gratitude to my mom, Maria Campbell, for her love, support, guidance and encouragement over the years; to Patrick Lane and Lorna Crozier — I am especially grateful for their love, humour and sound advice; to my many writer friends, including Joanne Arnott, Marilyn Dumont, Larissa Lai, Eden Robinson, Joe Walsh and many others whom I've failed to mention — forgive me.

Heartfelt thanks and gratitude to my best friend, Kelli Speirs, who has been there since the beginning; Annabel Webb; Janine Humphreys; Carol Kellmen; Melanie Speirs; Candace Gordon; Bernice Hammersmith; Mary Weigers and Maurie Cunningham. Love and thanks to all.

Love to my sisters Roxanne, Tanice and Cyndy; my brother Dan; my cousins Holly and Colin; and Virginia Houle-Bernier. These poems and songs are our legacy. To Aunty Donna, who is both my mother and friend: I love you.

Blessings to my Aunty Georgina's family: Felix Houle, Eva Erickson, Caroline Houle and her many nieces and nephews.

I gratefully acknowledge the BC Arts Council and The Canada Council for their generous support.

Finally, blessings to all of you, my readers — may these poems and songs fill your heart with pride.

In friendship,
Gregory Scofield

"I guess you got no business with the blues unless you can sing 'em ... "

— Jimmie Rodgers, from *Down The Old Road*

EARLY COUNTRY FAVOURITES

Keep on the sunny side
Always on the sunny side,
Keep on the sunny side of life.
It will help us every day
It will brighten all the grey
If we keep on the sunny side of life …
        — The Carter Family, "Keep On the
           Sunnyside," from *Mid The Green*
           Fields of Virginia

PICTURE 1 (1973)

She always wore a flower,
an orchid, lily
a spray of wild buttercups
tucked behind her ear

dancing
around the house
like a Hawaiian princess
in her floral-print dress,
something she'd picked up
from Sally Ann,
cut and altered
to hide her white legs.

One time,
I caught the backside of her
running to the bathroom.
Later, I teased her
about her white bum,
about seeing France
without her pants.

"I-yee!" she scolded,
waving her hand,

the same hand
that kneaded bannock dough,

threaded needles and beads,

picked fleas off the dog,

scratched the needle on records,

hovered above Harry,
when love was a garden,
when times, not so ugly,
waltzed her feet without music.
Her hand landing soft,
like petals from her hair.

HEART FOOD

for Marilyn Dumont

Pine-Sol is the smell of home
where handmade curtains
trimmed with lace
warmed winter windows, where

baking bread, loaves fat and soft
as pillows,
hung under my nose, woke
my tastebuds

to stewing moose meat
and whipped potatoes,
kissed my lips
with sweet apple or cherry pie,

where mugs of hot tea
heaped with sugar, evaporated milk,
were later slurped at the table
strewn with glass beads,

flower templates and moccasin tongues,
scraps of smoked moose hide
tanned out back of Caroline's place
and sent from Alberta

with old slacks, sweaters
and blouses
that no longer fit, that hemmed
and altered became like new,

new like the second-hand dolls
she washed and dressed
in miniature petticoats, perfectly stitched
dresses and boots

who jigged on the shelf
to fiddle tunes, whose tiny hands
clapped along to records
or conducted

her guitar songs
long after I fell to sleep,
the smell of Pine-Sol,
smoked moose hide, cinnamoned apples

etching their way
silently into my knowing,
running deeper than the blood
feeding my heart.

MOOSHOM, A SUNG HERO

Though he died two years
before I was born,

growing up
he was a sung hero, sung

happy-go-lucky
as robins in spring

so his laugh
skipped along to records,
his eyes
winked from pictures
Mom brought to life,

her fingers waltzing
guitar strings, accordion keys
polished as his wedding band
she'd cut down,
sized to fit her own finger
where it stayed
regardless of who came along
or talked a good line.

"He'll always be
my number one," she'd say, two-stepping with his ghost
humming in her ear,

humming "The Old Rugged Cross"
or fiddle tunes
from *Don Messer's Jubilee*.

The day he died, she told me,
a black cloud hung over the house,
spilling the tears of angels
hovering up high, watching
as he rolled a cigarette,
dug in his old leather change purse
for his last nickel,

his once-busted nose
sniffing Heaven's barroom
where Cheechum and her gang
sat waiting, waiting

like me at Mom's bedside later
waiting for them to come,
to call her

up and out of herself,
guide her home
where the music is all original,
the beer cold
and two-steps are perfect
like floating clouds.

She always said
I looked just like him,

had the same gold heart
and that

made me damn proud.

    Mooshom: Grandfather
    Cheechum: Great Grandmother

MEMORIES OF A WABASCA GIRL

She'd saddle up Blacky,
shoot away
like a rodeo rider, red-cheeked
and trotting
down the lonesome trail,
crooning
the wind into song, harmonizing to the Jack pine,
spruce and poplar,

sweetly lulling the waves
into chorus
on North Wabasca Lake,
yodelling the pale sky blue,
swirling the clouds
like a lariat
rounding up the sunset,
chords of burnt orange and red
strummed by God's own guitar,

the fat stars of twilight
falling far over the hill
like drunkards,
happily slumped together
under the moon's silver glow
snoring till sun-up,
her last song homeward.

OH, DAT AGNES

Wuk-wa, Aunty would roar
between chipped teeth
and slap her leg
so the dogs jumped and barked.

You know, she told me,
Her fadder was a Swede, uh.
But boy, coult she ever
speak goot Cree.

One dime
we hat to glean dah ghapel
an I says to her,
"Hey Agnes, I wonder
what dah fadder's always drinkin?"

"I dunno," she says,
shruckin hers shoulders like dis.

"Well, it must be goot," I says,
"cause hees always drinkin it.
Maybe we shoult try some, uh?"

"Oh my, Georgie," she says
makin a fat kokoos face.
"Mmm ... dis is goot."

"Wa, mucheementow!" I says to her
an crabbed dat chug o' wine.

Well dah next ting you know
we forget all about dah ghapel.

Den dat grazy ting started singin.
Boy oh boy,
shes sounded like a coddamn gat
howlin at dah moon.

Well, we finished off dat chug
an started on dah next one.

"Hey, what about dis song?" I says.

"I ton't gare what dey say
all dah mooneeyas iskwaysuk
keetasay …"

Well, dat Agnes
was laughin so hart
she farted an falled over.

Holy gripe, next ting you know
dat Sister Tennis

game chargin up to dah alter
an says,
"Hey, you geerls!
What's going on in here!"

An dat was dat.
Boy, did we ever gatch hell.
Hers dad laughed about it, dough,
toll everyone
we got trunk on Ghrist's blood.

Wuk-wa, mucheementowuk! she'd chuckle,
lighting another cigarette.

An dere was dah dime we …

Wuk-wa: *Oh my goodness*
Kokoos: *Pig*
Wa, mucheementow: *Oh my, you devil*
Mooneeyas iskwaysuk keetasay: *All the white girls take
        down their pants*
Mucheementowuk: *Devils*

A JIG FOR SISTER

Aunty got slapped
one too many times,

yanked around by her hair
like a rag doll,

squeezed or pinched
told to hurry up, shut up

in Mass or the dining hall.
It was that Sister Dennis,

French right to the core
and mean as a wolverine

just sniffing for any reason
to hiss and snap

God's word, her clapper
or booted feet

coming down the hallway
or up three flights of stairs.

One time, Aunty said,
this young girl was bleeding

for the first time
and Sister dragged her

from the bed, marched her
up to the altar

in her soiled nightgown,
pointing and screaming,

"You dirty thing!
You filthy, filthy girl!"

Another time, she said,
she was late putting on her shoes.

Already the other girls
were lined up for breakfast.

Sister grabbed her, pushed her
into place, yelling rules

so even the brothers outside
stopped to listen.

What she said
was a flash of red

blood red
blew up in Aunty's face

and her hands like a badger's
snarled around Sister's neck,

pushed her to the floor
so the girls screamed,

"Pukamow, Georgina! Pukamow!"

but in the end
her floating fist opened

smacked Sister's face
so the sound was a horse whip

and Sister, holding her bald head,
ran from the room

muttering prayers in French,
dragging her veil, her busted rosary.

Later, Mother Superior said
such evil acts

wouldn't be tolerated.
"I'm sixteen," Aunty said,

turning on her moccasined heels,
cross-jigging out the door.

Pukamow! Pukamow!: Hit her! Hit her!

TWO CRADLE-SONGS

Mom

As long as I remember,
north, south, east
or west

houses, apartments or shacks,
roads winding endless miles
or streets

wet with rain, drumming
sad in the night
and me to sleep

she'd rub my back,
draw letters that spelled
GREG or LOVE

comb my hair with fingers
that'd counted change,
the days till Christmas

or my birthday, the hours
till dawn, lulling my heart
even now, her song

safe, assuring as ever,

> *Shoo-shoo-shoo-sha-la-la*
> *Put your little cares away*
> *Shoo-shoo-shoo-sha-la-la*
> *Tomorrow is a another day*
> *Shoo-shoo-shoo-sha-la-la*
> *Close your little eyes so blue*
> *Shoo-shoo-shoo-sha-la-la*
> *Pretty dreams will come to you …*

> — Wilf Carter, "Shoo She Lah Lah,"
> from *Wilf Carter, Montana Slim*

Aunty

No matter how
young or old,
sober, half-cut
or gone

she'd fluff the pillows,
spread and tuck
her homemade quilts
under my chin,

count the patches in Cree
starting sometimes at nine,
ten to see if I was listening,
if I'd laugh and say,
"Keeskwiyan,"
just the way she taught me,
mischievously,
knitting my brows together,
mouth tight and puckered
so she'd say,
"Ma, tapway chee?"

"E-he," I'd nod
and wait, the song
a bluebird on her lips
lifting me to dreams

    Sleep baby sleepy
    Close your bright eyes
    Listen to your mother, dear
    Sing these lullabies.
    Sleep baby sleepy
    While angels watch over you
    Listen to your mother, dear
    While she sings to you …

        — Jimmie Rodgers, from re-recorded
          cassette by Georgina Houle Young

Keeskwiyan: You're crazy
Ma, tapway chee?: Oh my, is that right?
E-he: Yes

HONKY TONKIN'

It wasn't God who made
Honky Tonk angels
As you said in the words
Of your song.
Too many times married men
Think they're still single
And it's led many a good gal
To go wrong ...

— Kitty Wells, "It Wasn't God Who
Made Honky Tonk Angels," from
Kitty Wells' Greatest Hits

AUNTY, LEFT TO HER RESOURCES

It was damn Harry
who got her going.

That's how it always happened,
'cause he wanted to run around.

"Old bugger," she'd say,
piling the beer into the fridge
as he slipped out,
drinking the first one on ice.

But after a while
the hands on the clock
didn't care
and really, neither did she.

Hers were busy
plucking the strings
up and down,

filling the house with songs
that spilled out onto the street
and infiltrated sleeping ears.

Like Harry,
even the cops knew
not to come knocking

two days later.

RIGHT TO DAH SUN-UP

Oh, she'd crab dat guitar
like a lover, yup

crab heem by dah neck
an pluck hees strinks, tapway

just like dat, strummin
along to dah Garter Family,

makin heem howl
dah whole night trough,

gordin up an town hees spine
till hees chumpin over dah moon

an dah stars climmer
an shine

like dah iyz
of dat Mudder Maybelle,

all dose saints
who shined on dah Opry

kiyas or on dah radio
up nort in dah push, yup

she'd crab dat guitar, twang
bluer den blue

howling to dah sun-up
den wake hers old man, yodelling,

"Daddy, I gotta pee
an dah gats got to go outsite."

tapway: for sure
kiyas: a long time ago
Mudder Maybelle: Mother Maybelle Carter from
    the Carter Family

T. FOR

Texas, T. for Tennessee,
T. for Texas, T. for Tennessee,
T. for Thelma
That gal that made
A wreck out of me

If you don't want me mama,
You sure don't have to stall,
Lord, Lord,
If you don't want me mama,
You sure don't have to stall
'Cause I can get more women
Than a passenger train can haul …

and the needle would catch,
slide into
its well-worn groove,
refusing to budge
like Fat Paul the bootlegger
our very own
small-town Buddha.

Even weighted with pennies
and promises
it wouldn't move
so T. was always for Texas,
Tennessee, for Thelma
that invisible gal
that made a wreck
out of the record, so

T. ended up
strummed in D, sung in C minor
D. for Desmarais, Alberta,
C. for the Carter Family
and Harry ...

If you don't want me daddy
You sure don't have to call,
If you don't want me daddy
You sure don't have to call,
Cause I can get more neecheemoosuk
than a dog sled can haul

and the needle and Fat Paul
scratched
and waited, stubborn
as hell,
thinking it was damn funny
till they
both got busted.

> — lyrics sung by Jimmie Rodgers, "Blue Yodel
> No. 1," from *Down the Old Road*

neecheemoosuk: sweethearts

THE LAST TIME LILLIAN CARDINAL
CAME TO VISIT

She was Aunty's old-time chum,
the sister
of her first boyfriend.

"Dat was almost
my sister-in-law," she'd say
when she talked
about their old school days.

That time
Lilly got the bus out
from the city,
stepped off smiling
as wide as the brim
on Hank's hat.

That time
she brought her guitar,
marched it proudly
into the house
like a new husband.

"Wak-wa, Lilly. Kiyas," Aunty said,
her brows knitted together.
"I see you brought yer olt man, uh?"

"Eee," Lilly chided, nudging her,
"Where he goes, I go."

Three nights
they strummed and cooed.
The beer bottles
piled up on the counter,
left dark circles on the table
and under their eyes.

> *Oh, the school house that stands upon the hill*
> *I never, never can forget,*
> *Dear happy days*
> *I gather round me still,*
> *I never, oh, never can forget ...*

The day she left
an owl hooted outside.
Sure enough,
two days later
the call came.

And Aunty,
diligent as the moon,
nursed doubles,
played every scratched record

in the house,
strumming up all the ghosts
they'd drank to, singing

lonesome
as heaven's angels
lifting Lilly and her guitar
back home.

Wak-wa, Lilly. Kiyas: Oh my goodness, Lilly.
It's been a long time

— lyrics sung by The Carter Family,
"The School House On The Hill,"
from *Lonesome Pine Special*

BLUE MOON

His lonesome yodel was really
Aunty's call disguised
As a cowboy song,
Lulling the stars, pulling down

The old Kentucky moon
So sad and drear
As she rolled along
Inside the living room,

Left tears
On the kitchen floor,
Rubbing memories
From her swollen eyes.

No wonder
She took to drinking
Beer, wine — anything
For a moment's peace,
Any reason
To sit and sing
How the stars made her blue,
How tired she was

Scrubbing heaven's floor
Or holding up the thankless sky
Right from the snow-covered prairie
To the blue Canadian Rockies

And her old man, the sun,
So damn lazy
There was no point getting up
But to stay up

The whole night through,
Three records on the turntable
Scratched all to hell
But good company anyway.

Still, the blues set in
More years than ninety-nine.
Once, God told her
He did make honky tonk angels

And giving them a drink
Was only proper,
Like Sunday Service.
But I never heard a hymn

Like her and Jimmie
Singing side by side
Down the old road
Home.

> — "Ninety-Nine Year Blues" by Jimmie Rodgers,
>   from *Down the Old Road*

GOING TO GET UNCLE

The cops showed up that time
escorting Uncle
and his damn good shiner
to pack some things.

"Shh, kiya keepeekiskweet,"
she whispered,
shaking her head
like an old time chief
so as not to sign the treaty
or give away
the last buffalo,
unlike Uncle
who hummed and hawed,
skittered about,
grabbing the clock,
dirty tea towels and socks.

"Wa, puksees!" she rasped
when no one was looking,
an invisible thread
sewing her lips
into a smirk.

After,
I asked how he got
the puffed eye.

"He falled on dah goffee dable,"
she said, stacking the empties
back in their case.

"Hmm ... must have had help,"
I said, a little elder
chewing my top lip.

Her laughter shattered the silence
like the beer bottle in the sink.

"Well," she confessed,
"dat ole bugger hat it comin.
Wants to run aroun
night an day. So boom!
I let heem have it
right on hees fat face."

"Ann-tee!" I protested,
"No wonder he brought the cops."

"Ah, never mind," she said,
waving her hand.
"To hell wit heem."

But by noon
we sat on her bed
in front of the mirror
and the transformation began.

Sober as a judge,
she brushed the knots
from her hair,
rolling it into a bun.
The paint — "her warpaint,"
she called it —
brought her lips and cheeks
back to life.
And finally,
a few quick Avon sprays
to appease the gods.

Rummaging through the fridge
a sandwich was made
from leftovers,
sliced cheese and pickles
and one stray
blueberry bannock.

"Blue bannock for dah blue eye,"
she chuckled, heading out the door.
"Dah bugger will like dat."

Shh, kiya keepeekiskweet: Shh, don't say anything
Wa, puksees!: Oh God, the mouse!

NO MESSING AROUND

Anyone the least bit smart
Knows messing with her
Is to disturb a spring bear
Nursing her cubs,
Is to contemplate
Feeding a cougar garbage —
Or be foolish enough to feed it.

Once, at the Haney Hotel,
She took on three women
Single-handedly in the can.
One took a plunge
In the toilet, one
Got a gut-ache for a keepsake,
The other, a busted lip
Fat as her stories.

"Yup," she says,
Pointing to the blue moon
Under her eye.
"Dah mouthy one did dis to me.
But holy gripe! You know Aunty, uh!"

"Bham!" she shoots,
The bullet smoking from her mouth,
Chest puffed up,

Her fist
Landing the imaginary face
In her palm.

She looks up, mischievous
As Wesakeejack
Spinning his tall tales.
"Tapway," she grins,
"No wooman mess around wit me."

"Ah, mucheementow," I scold
To her laughter,

Though growing up
How many times I wished
She'd come to school,
Hand-talk the bully.

> *Wesakeejack: Cree trickster*
> *Tapway: It's true*
> *Mucheementow: Devil*

PICTURE 2: THE VIGIL (1974)

Mom's long-gone lonesome blues
wobbled and scratched
round the turntable, heart heavy

and glum
like the rain pining outside,
crackling
her old memories
through the speakers,

her sweet love lost
twenty-odd years
but she still dreaming

of days gone by, bush
and mud
dried like her countless tears
warping
the yellowed pictures
she kept in her wallet —

his picture,
holding me,
proud as any papa, grinning
as if I were his own,

as if their world
would never change,
the north
would stay forever legendary,
distant and invisible
like the wolves who howled
black nights

endless now with the rain
tapping her windows, down south

where she always kept
a light burning.

HOME ON THE RANGE

Oh, how my lonely heart is aching tonight
For a home I long to see,
And oh, what I'd give
If I could be there tonight
With a sweetheart who's waiting for me …
　　— Wilf Carter, "Blue Canadian Rockies,"
　　　from *God Bless Our Canada*

PICTURE 3 (1979)

She was never the type
to pose in silk or fur.

Wore an old Stetson
steamed over a pot
on the stove
and tied to keep its shape,
like the hats of the old-timers
who debuted on the Opry
and later
signed her songbooks.

My friends saw
gold crosses and pearls
drape their mothers' necks,
saw sparkling jewels
render their hands
useless but pretty.

Mine was proud
to clomp down the street
in boots,
happy as hell to show off
her silver and turquoise hatband,
Grandpa's wedding ring
with its one sad diamond,

the two gold saddles
that swung from her lobes
minus their riders.

In school
I was embarrassed
of the Indian cowboy who sidled up to the front door
revving her station wagon,
bumper hanging
like the mouths
that would ask,
"Who's that?"

It wasn't until my late teens,
until someone said,
"Is that your mom or dad?"
that I told the truth.

Now all the white kids
want Indian moms
wearing big glasses and hats,
riding old Pinto
hatchbacks
from the junkyard,
tapping their toes
to Wilf and Hank
on the rigged-up radio.

1975-1978

It didn't matter
we lived
down by the river,
stayed at
the Fraser Valley Hotel
eight months

or ate from
the Chinese corner store.

It didn't matter
she stayed out late
A.A. meeting nights

or I stayed up
munching chips
in front of the TV

It didn't matter
we moved
closer to the river,
dodged crazies
at the Marlo Apartments

or drug addicts
flying from the roof.

It didn't even matter
that she fell off the wagon,
charged up bottles
from Fat Paul
till cheque day.

She drank at home
and no one came around.

What mattered
was the ex-cop
who took us kids for ice-cream,
whose hands
strayed beneath our swim trunks
when no one was looking.

It was little Danny
who finally
spilled the beans.

First time
I ever saw her
spitting and wild —

only time
I ever heard her say
she'd kill the bastard
if it weren't for jail

or losing me.

I NEVER DID LEARN TO SAY

for Roxanne, my sister

> *We were poor but we had love,*
> *That's the one thing*
> *My daddy made sure of,*
> *He shoveled coal*
> *To make a poor man's dollar …*
> — Loretta Lynn, "Coal Miner's Daughter,"
>   from *Loretta Lynn's Greatest Hits*

Mine skipped out
six months
after I was born

a faceless figure
who co-wrote the story,
who didn't stick around
to hear the ending

or even the beginning.

His replacements
were drunks
or heavy-handed teachers.

I learned that walking
was to tip-toe, "yes"
the right answer,
that pillows plugged ears

and filtered screams.

Most of the time
it was just her and me,
two old veterans
who survived the words,
the wars

even the scars.

As for as being poor —
yes, we lived
in too many shacks to count.
Sure there were drafts
and leaks, peeling linoleum
and cracked walls.

But love was always
at her fingertips,
spreading scatter-rugs, doilies

and music to grow up on,
so the story came to life,
a life I wouldn't change.

I never did learn
to say, "Dad."
It was a foreign word
practiced only in my head

simple enough,
but always
those three barbed-wire letters
poked, drew blood
from the tip of my tongue.

RED DEVIL

She made him
in the loony bin
after the dreams started —

just the head, a goat's head
with hollow eyes,
a pointed chin
and two perfect horns.

Still
his hooves clomped
at night
and his tail flickered
at the foot of her bed,
snakes slithering
from his mouth.

The doctors diagnosed
delusions of Christian guilt,
hooked electrodes to her head
so angels would sing,
sweep their wings
where lizards crawled.

But God saw everything —

the silver sparks
eating up her brain, chewing
the memories
so when the social worker
shoved a form under her nose,
told her to sign me away,

he worked her lips
into the shape of no

and the devil laughed
at how they saved her tongue
with a mouthguard.

Two years later
she came to get me.

Once I was digging
through the dresser
and found him rolled up
in an old sock.

He looked as sinister
as ever, grinning
right from the core
of his poisoned head.

One horn was busted
and she told me
to put it back,
to never unwrap him again.

Now he lives
in my top drawer,
cursing my underwear and socks.
If it wasn't for God
and all her lost memories
I'd smash him to pieces —
but some blackness
is better left in the dark.

LITTLE GOLD JESUS

He originally came from the convent school,
that little gold figure
so sad and frail
from being packed around
all those miles,
from being taped and re-taped
to his wooden cross.

Aunty didn't say
how he'd broken at the wrists
and ankles,
only that she'd be damned
if he got down.

Still, everywhere she went
he hung above the bed.
His bent head
never once looked up,
even when she won bingo
or had a few too many.

At night
I used to watch him,
waiting like a cat
for him to break free.
His hands and feet

were still nailed
and I wondered
how he'd manage a safe landing.

"Aunty," I asked one time,
"How come he's busted?"
"Cause he was tryin
to wiggle off," she smirked,
more for the nuns
than for me.

The day she died
I wrapped him up in tissue paper
and brought him home.
I even bought some crazy glue.
But in the end
I gave him a good smudge
and more tape.

THEY TAUGHT HER
for Louise, Sky-Dancer

praying, bruised on the knees,
was the right way,
that God, an old whiteman,
only heard
Hail Marys, Our Fathers.

They taught her

how to make beds,
thick bread and whipped potatoes,
where to put the plates,
knives and forks,

where the pleats go
in Father's slacks, his robe
for Mass,
where the candles are set,
the chalice and bell,
what to polish them with.

They taught her

French was civilized
and even holy things in Cree
didn't compare,

that nicknames for the Sisters
were like swearing at God
or vandalizing the church,

that Breeds
were halfway to being redeemed
and praying extra hard
would open Heaven's gate.

They taught her

all boys had the devil's snake
and kissing on the keemootch
would put a bun in the oven,
land her in purgatory or hell
where she'd spend her days
fanning fires, picking lice
from the heads of demons.

By sixteen

they taught her

being a good wife
was to take it
on the chin, in the eye

73

or gut
even if the bun was half-baked.

The first baby
left blood in her panties,
an ache in her stomach,
then emptiness.

Father said
it was meant to be,
that forgiveness
was God's own teaching.

The other babies, well —
she didn't say.
That's another story.

on the keemootch: on the sly or sneaky

OLD PAL OF MINE

> *You are my sunshine, my only sunshine,*
> *You make me happy*
> *When skies are gray,*
> *You'll never know, dear,*
> *How much I love you,*
> *Please don't take my sunshine away …*
>> — Wilf Carter, "You Are My Sunshine,"
>> from *Wilf Carter, Montana Slim*

I remember
Mom and Marv
at the kitchen table
rolling cigarettes,

sharing drinks,
and long silences
that passed between them
undisturbed

lifted to haziness
overhead
like the blue smoke
from the ashtray, between them

not a bloody nickel
till cheque day.

"Kind as a saint," she always said
after he left, leaving behind
the smell
of other peoples' junk
that slipped into the walls,
burrowed into her carpets.

He never said much
when I came around, though once
he gave me
a warped coffee table
he'd stored in
old lady Macky's garage.

I only guessed
her change of life
dulled her need
for men — really any need
for them at all.

A few old geezers
she drank with
at the Army and Navy Club
teased her,
said she could do better.

"Whatever you think," she'd say,
shrugging her shoulders,
laughing behind her glasses.

Most times
they just sat, listening
to her old records,
Marv's eyes dozing off
like her dog
at his feet.

"Go on," she'd softly chide.
"I fixed you a bed
on the couch." And he'd sleep
and sleep, his snoring
shaking her walls, her nerves,
so I'd hear about it
the day after.

Then one day
he dropped by, announced
he was shacking up
with the German woman
we all knew
wasn't right in the head.

Her husband
had blown his brains out
after the war, something
Mom explained to me
as God's justice.

Nonetheless
they visited often,
all of them
drinking and smoking —
that woman
talking non-stop,
Mom and Marv
quiet as church mice.

The day after Mom's funeral
I walked down to the river,
to the hotel
where they lived.

"I sure loved your mom," he said,
his voice thin and hollow
as if his words
had blown in from a canyon
on a sad wind.

"She loved you, too," I said,
handing him her cigarette roller,
can of tobacco
and tubes.

CUT-OFF

A month's worth of piled-up bottles,
heaped-up ashtrays
and records strewn

and Aunty would cut them off,
set to scrubbing the floors
and walls, Harry's clothes,
and blankets
used by the multitudes
who'd come for one drink,
ended up toasting
always one more
to the wild roses of Alberta
or dogwoods
that sagged outside
from lack of sleep.

It always happened
quick as a rain storm
after lightning.
Suddenly she'd burst,
smashing her fist on the table,

half sober, thunder
rumbling from her mouth,
"Look at all dese goddamn people
hangin aroun in here!"

Harry was the first to get it.
The whole month
he'd made cameo appearances,
snuck home to change
or eat — seldom to sleep
if he got an invite
from one of the women
he played around with.

There'd be
three months of perfect silence,
hot tea and bannock.
We'd sit up late
making animal shadows
dance across the wall.
Harry dozed in front of the TV
oblivious to the language
our animals spoke.

Then sure enough,
Christmas would come
bringing memories of her son John.
A bottle would arrive
like a new baby,

and in no time
all the well-wishers
to cheer her on.

LONESOME PINE SPECIAL

I don't hurt anymore
All my teardrops are dried;
No more walkin' the floor
With that burnin' inside
Just to think it could be,
Time has opened the door
And at last I am free …

       — Hank Snow, "I Don't Hurt Anymore,"
         from *Souvenirs*

DOWN SOUTH

One day I came home
to find Grandmother
packing the house.

"We're going down south," she said,
stuffing the north
into boxes bigger than me.

I never thought to ask,
even when my sister Brenda
didn't return from school.

Later, on the plane,

I remembered my muskrat mittens —
the soft puppets
I dragged around
had escaped their only family.

The first tear came,
then another and another
until my face
was a swollen cloud
over Miles Canyon.

I was six.
Six and not tasting
the sandwich made
the night before.
Six
in the small bones of my hand
that clung to Grandmother,
that ached from the rain
down south.

But farther south
behind the locked doors
of Hollywood Hospital,
Mom convulsed like a gasping fish,
the north, the midnight sun,
forgotten like the land, the land
of howling wolves and singing stars
to which she'd never return.

BLUE EYES

Rusty came from Smith, Alberta,
a terrier cross,
smart as hell.
Aunty got him after John died,
a gift
from Georgina Nipshank
to keep her company,
to ease the infinite pain
I would one day
come to know.

I was seven
and thought death
was like a movie hero
who, Mom assured me,
got up and walked around later.

But Aunty knew different.
Already, her first two boys
were walking another set
and hadn't been written
back into the script.

Those ones
she seldom talked about,
even when drinking.

But John
she talked about all the time.
He was only thirty-two,
and coming home for Christmas.
The car was so smashed
he was barely recognizable.

Once she pulled out
his old sketches and cards.
I fingered them
as if I were touching dust.
Lifting the beer to her lips,
she squinted through her glasses.
"My boy," she said, "like you
he hat dah most beaudiful blue iyz."

Long into many nights
she would sit telling stories,
Rusty at her feet,
dozing.
Sometimes
for no reason
the lights would flicker
and he would jump to attention,
howl as if grabbed.

Once
a silhouette
stood at the foot of my bed.
"Take care of Mom," he said,
passing through the wall.

I told Aunty.
She hugged me close.

HALF THE STORY

Over the years

it wasn't clear

how

Aunty's Mom died ... Something to do with fire

in the middle of winter
in a cabin
somewhere between Slave Lake
and Athabasca.

Just the two of them
in that goddamn place,
the old lady
and someone visiting.

It wasn't clear

if

by some chance

they were drinking, if

the wood stove spit flames
or kerosene leaked
by accident.

Nonetheless,
the old lady and her friend
burnt to the bloody ground.

Aunty never said much —

only that it was forty below,
and the old lady
was a damn good Christian
in her day.

HALF OF ANOTHER STORY

They told me Aunty died
from a poisoned liver,
from the blood clot in her head,
from falling.

They assured us
it was accidental.

Harry said, "Oh yes,
she was drunk and fell."
The cops
took it to be gospel,
didn't bother
taking statements
from Virgie or me.

But two days before,
his thin voice had quavered
on my answering machine,
a skinny willow
about to bust.

I knew then, knew it
sure as a wolf knows
the hunter's trap,
how to chew off his foot
to survive.

Now her ghost
pokes in the kitchen at night
and the dog's ears
perk
at every sound.

Last night
I found out this guy
named Roy
had raped her a few years ago.
He ripped her so bad
she had to be sewn up
and Harry took money
to keep her mouth shut.

He doesn't think I know

but I do.

I know the whole story,
black as night
and crow's wings
that flutter her words
in my sleep,

that hover outside and speak
the silences
of many mouths drunk

on her wine.

THEY SAW

a bag lady, a rag woman
barely held together
by her bones

They saw

scuffed boots that'd tromped
so many goddamn miles
and still had the wherewithal
to make it
to the beer and wine store
before closing

They saw

how she picked over
the bargain jeans at Zellers,
how for the tenth time
she didn't need their help,
them hovering
just in case she might

They saw her

perfumed as all hell,
wafting into the bank
on cheque day,
and barely spoke two words to her
thinking she wouldn't understand,
or worse yet, she'd be drunk.
One time, she said, a woman
whispered behind her back,
"Just look where our tax
dollars are going."

And they saw

what all their parents said —
Indian women her age
were walking corpses
scrounging for a drink

But

one of the last times
I saw her
she was coming down the road,
those boots
clomping like horse hooves
one in front of the other,
dragging a bag of groceries,
a few stray beer cans
rolling at the bottom

I saw her

my patch-quilt mother
with a hat so beat up
only a miracle
kept it on her head.
Running to meet her,
I saw her eyes charm up a smile.
"Look!" she said,
glowing in her new sweatshirt:
METIS & PROUD OF IT.

TOO MANY BLUEBERRIES

I've seen

Their eyes
So black and blue
Not even wet rocks
Compare, hold a flame

To the bones
I've heard snap, crack
And bust
Like skinny twigs

Beneath an evil eye
Or heavy hand
That kept them in line,
In place

If ever their mouths
Ran overboard,
Spilled the truth,
Not always drinking truth

But God's truth,
His own goddamn truth
That was better a lie,
A white lie

Stretched over years
To cover their mouths,
Shape them into smiles
So the cops and doctors never asked
If ribs didn't heal, if berries
collected beneath the skin

But

I've seen them
So black and blue
Not even purple was a
Recognizable colour,
Their eyes swollen shut
So that even crying was hard,
And puddles welled up, dried
Without ever forming tears

Yet

I've heard them say
Not to worry, not to hate.
But I carry their bones,
Their tears

Like a basket of berries,
Blue and heavy,
Rotting black
Like crows hovering

Till the last gets picked.

SHE'S LIVED

ten lives, ten beat-up lives,
ten thousand years

in the Safeway parking lot,
feeding her dogs
from the dumpster,

holed-up
in her station wagon,
no place to go.

She's lived

in old meat trucks,
converted them into home,
tacked up pictures
scattered rag rugs and treasures
so you could smell
her old memories.

She's lived

in town, rented shacks
from the municipality,

from white landlords
who never fixed the heat
or the stove that leaked gas
and gave her headaches

ten thousand years.

She's lived

day to day,
hocked her guitar
to pay the hydro, buy tobacco,
a few cold beers
to wash down
all the things
she wasn't supposed to say,
bitch or complain about
when she got evicted
because someone's mother or daughter
needed a place
or the rent got jacked up

jacked up so high
she'd leave, take her dogs
back to the parking lot,

eating cold beans
by the interior light,

reading by flashlight
about stars who got facelifts
or landed cozy deals
or what her horoscope said,
though it never came true.

The truth was

she lived

ten lives, ten thousand years,

prehistoric
and yet to be discovered.

One day
her forty-eight-year-old bones
simply gave up

and no one batted an eye.

NOT ALL HALFBREED MOTHERS
for Mom, Maria

Not all halfbreed mothers

drink

red rose, blue ribbon,
Kelowna Red, Labatt's Blue.

Not all halfbreed mothers
wear cowboy shirts or hats,
flowers behind their ears
or moccasins
sent from up north.

Not all halfbreed mothers
crave wild meat,
settle for hand-fed rabbits
from SuperStore.

Not all halfbreed mothers
pine over lost loves,
express their heartache
with guitars, juice harps,

old records shoved
into the wrong dustcover.

Not all halfbreed mothers
read *The Star*, *The Enquirer*,
The Tibetan Book of the Dead
or Edgar Cayce,
know the Lady of Shalott
like she was a best friend
or sister.

Not all halfbreed mothers
speak like a dictionary
or Cree hymn book,
tell stories
about faithful dogs
or bears
that hung around or sniffed
in the wrong place.

Not all halfbreed mothers
know how to saddle
and ride a horse,
how to hot-wire a car
or siphon gas.

Not all halfbreed mothers

drink

red rose, blue ribbon,
Kelowna Red, Labatt's Blue.

Mine just happened
to like it

Old Style.

TRUE NORTH, BLUE COMPASS HEART

Twenty-eight years, drenched to the bone
she talked about Wabasca,
the old days, mud-caked roads
and muskeg forever

a blue compass heart
pointing north, lost
like moose tracks
in the snow

on this wet, grey coast
where other women like her —
true bush and tough —
outlasted city streets,

phantom whitewomen
who floated ever so delicately
behind shaded windows,
drinking herbal tea,
poisoning their children
neatly to sleep.

She told me of a place
in Wabasca
so sacred it couldn't be named,
a clearing in the bush

thick with Jack pine, spruce,
moss earth beneath her feet.

One time, she said,
she got lost.
Still as the dead
she stood there and was lifted,
carried like a leaf
to the road back home.

"Seepwaypiyow," the old people said
and this became her name,
stuck long after
TB ate her lungs, long after
the sanatorium closed
and the Wabasca, the people,
the wild roses of her childhood,
became stories
that skipped across the kitchen table,
sung over strong tea
brewed in a blue enamel pot.

One night
we were out walking, picking cans.
"Hey, you fucking squaw!" some kids
yelled from a car.

"Never mind," she said,
taking my small hand.

I don't remember getting home.
Only that we were
standing on the steps,
all the lights burning inside.

Down south
she joked about snaring rabbits,
checking her trapline
which in the end
ran through the cemetery,
grew wild with clovers, dogwoods

over her
a plot of hard earth
sinking and settling,
claiming the north, the sun
in a distant land

spooked with strangers.

Seepwaypiyow: She flies away

MOM, AS I WATCHED HER LEAVING

became small so very small
as she laboured
her whole eighty pounds
to catch one breath thin as

the sound of my voice
drifting above her,
lost vowels
falling and landing
like snowflakes in a storm,
muted

as the tubes
invading her body, resonating
what was first ingested air,
a wailing song then scream
as the stretch and tear
of my wet head
poked out
and knew by instinct
her language, though frail

and now receding
like the owl
who flutters his wings
beneath her eyes, birthing tears

from a place
beyond my knowing,

beyond the cord which binds me
to those who wait
at the foot of her bed, calling,
"Dorothy, peekeewe, peekeewe,"
in a language
I can neither hear nor understand

though each muscle, every cell
of my being
contracts and strains
like the cold fingers
which pull her from my grasp,
struggle
against my every promise.

But in the end the final moment
I bend to her ear, offer
my own breath
which comes deep and prosperous

sing
my twenty-six years
of memories and songs,

knowing for the first time
life as solitary as death.

And she hears. She hears
as the world closes,
swallows my every vowel,
cuts my every chord releasing

her to a place
where all language
is obsolete.

peekeewe, peekeewe: come home, come home

PICTURE 4 (1995)

On the wall, on the wall
How I love
That dear old picture
On the wall.
Time is swiftly passing by
And I bow my head and cry
Cause I know
I'll meet my mother after all ...
        — The Carter Family, "Picture On The Wall,"
           from *Mid the Green Fields of Virginia*

Her shoulders raised and
Stooped over the guitar
Crooked in her arms,
Head a sway, hand a strum

Each finger a sail
Up, down, up, down again
Picking six tuned strings
So a thousand caught wind,

Rose up like blue/grey smoke
From the ashtray,
Summoning the notes from her belly
And filling

First her lungs, circling her heart,
Then up and out
Till each golden chord
Strung together became a song —

Her favourite
Old Carter Family tune
Or Cree love call
Or robins in spring,

Rolling hills or paintbrush
Sweeping the lonesome prairie,
Crooning the gophers
From their holes

Like me, a little lad
At her moccasined feet
Starry-eyed and dreaming
Angels above my head,

Cursing in my teens
Her guitar, her drinking music
That kept me tossing and turning
Wide-eyed

So bags hung
Black as bats, black and heavy
As the day
I stepped into her empty house,

Sat puff-eyed
At her table, waiting
As if she were asleep,
As if I'd missed her

By accident,
Overlooked her grocery shopping
Or visiting, misplaced her pick
So the silence, transparent

As a breath, infiltrated,
Settled into the cracks
Of my own heart, played without song
Like her guitar

Propped in the corner
Where she'd last left it,
Where her fingers pluck strings
I can no longer hear

Though I have one picture
Hanging on the wall,
Her head bent, eyes closed
So the song

Clear as wind on Wabasca Lake
Echoes, echoes and carries
Her from the frame
To someplace so wordless

Within.

Where is my wandering boy tonight
The boy of my tenderous care,
The boy that was once
My joy and light,
The child of my love and prayer,
Oh, where is my boy tonight …
      — Wilf Carter, "Where Is My Boy,"
        from *Let's Go Back to the Bible*

PICTURE 5 (1988)

She was damn proud
of that accordion.
Got it dirt cheap
from a pawn shop,

managed to lug it home
though it weighed
more than her.

The case, she said,
was beat to shit
but it didn't matter
cause you don't play
the case anyway.

At first
it sat in her lap
like a new baby,
keys carefully polished
and polished again
so its ivory and black teeth
gleamed beneath her fingers.

One time
she called it her squeeze box,
grinning so I got the joke.

"Mom!" I scolded, embarrassed,
as if sex
should be unknown, possibly
outlawed, to mothers.

"Well," she chided,
"at least I know how to play it."

But most times it sat
in the corner
taking second fiddle
to the guitar
she seldom put down.

Like Aunty, the guitar was her
one true love
who never got tired
or left for a younger,
smoother woman.

Their dueling guitars
were the twelve strings
I climbed to dreams on.

Once I overheard them
laughing downstairs.

"Hey, Dorothy," Aunty teased,
"how bout we warm up
dat squeeze box. She's lookin
a little lonely."

(HIGH) MASS, AND ONE GOOD BLUSHING

Sure as Joseph, she saw
the midnight star

and Christ himself
rolling in the aisle, snorting
and holding his gut

at her, flying high
with all the saints
so even the priest stopped

mid-blessing, cleared his throat
till her frog voice
halted the choir

somewhere between
silent and night,
the holy congregation

silent and staring
so a pine needle dropped
and was heard

from here to Jerusalem,
not in Hebrew or Latin
but in French, Quebecois

fur-trader French,
and Cree — her Christmas Cree
of tinselled syllables, bright vowels

brought to life
by dah tree wisemen
who'd dropped by earlier

bearing guitars and songs
and homemade wine,
so the chapel hush

was reason enough to start without the choir,
announce loudly
that she'd once been a nun,
and Mass — the goddamn thing
should be said entirely

in Cree and French,
with small children dressed as angels
and Christ Himself present

and rising up
like Harry Houdini
from the Great Beyond,

throwing down His cross
and up His arms,
like her, swatting me

in the front pew
to stop hushing her or telling her
not to yodel during communion.

"Ah! Dat's not even
Ghrist's body," she chided
to the woman next to her

as if she knew Him personally,
as if by some divine force
He spoke to her

while she wobbled down the aisle
wafer in hand, outstretched
to keep her steady.

Marching reverently
out the door
she turned to me,

faced scrunched up
so a hint of the devil
danced at the corners

of her lips, and spun me,
the usher, around,
mouth gaping and hot-cheeked

as I heard her say,
"I gotta place to go, anyway!"

PUT ME IN YOUR POCKET

All those years
Mom loved him, loved him
right to her last breath,
loved him
the way she loved
the north, the wild country
they'd wandered
in a beat-up car, us kids
packed neatly in the back
like the camping gear,
the many boxes
of clothes and food,
the map
that'd been folded and unfolded
so many times
it was a tired albatross
with torn wings
perfectly tucked into place
behind the visor.

She loved him
right to her last breath,
loved him
for each fading memory
she kept hidden
in her jewelry box —

the pictures of the land
being cut and cleared,
the house going up
like a haphazard skeleton,
and the unexpected shots:
scrubbing his longjohns,
our snotty noses
and plastic dishes.

Always, the smile she wore
was a schoolgirl's
in his arms.

She loved him
right to her last breath,
loved him
even in his silence
that echoed her every smile.
She loved him, loved him
long after her eyes closed
and there was only
the stale city smell
polluting her blood.

Going through her things
I found his picture, crying

from its tiny blue frame.
I had the undertaker
place him in the breast pocket
of her favourite coat.

That night I sat up,
incurably scratched and older
than the music
I grew up on.
Her records fanned the floor,
a grouse's tail
fluttering her into flight,
Wilf Carter cooing,

> *Put me in your pocket*
> *so I'll be close to you,*
> *No more will I be lonely and*
> *no more will I be blue,*
> *and when we have to part, dear,*
> *there'll be no sad adieu,*
> *For I'll be in your pocket*
> *and I'll go along with you …*

— Wilf Carter, "Put Me in your Pocket,"
from *Wilf Carter by Request*

DAH TING ABOUT WALTZING

is, she said,

never let dah wooman leet

cause if you do

she'll dake yer pants,

make you sign yer cheques

an hant dem over,

push you outta bet

to feet dah babies,

do dah dishes, if she wishes

make you hem her slacks,

go an get flour from dah store

to bake hers a gake,

ice dah damn ting, too.

Best ting, she said,

are dah ones

who step on yer does.

I'VE BEEN TOLD

Halfbreed heaven must be
handmade flowers of tissue,
poplar trees
forever in bloom,

the North and South Saskatchewan rivers
swirling and meeting
like the skirts, the hands
of cloggers
shuffling their moccasined feet.

I've been told

Halfbreed heaven must be
old Gabriel at the gate
calling, "Tawow! Tawow!"
toasting new arrivals, pointing
deportees
to the buffalo jump
or down the Great Canadian Railroad,
like Selkirk or MacDonald.

I've been told

Halfbreed heaven must be
scuffed floors and furniture
pushed to one side,
grannies giggling in the kitchen,
their embroidered hankies
teasing and nudging
the sweetest sweet sixteen,
who will snare the eye
of the best jigger.

I've been told

Halfbreed heaven must be
a wedding party
stretched to the new year,
into a wake, a funeral
then another wedding,
an endless brigade of happy faces
in squeaky-wheeled carts
loaded with accordions, guitars
and fiddles.

I've been told

Halfbreed heaven must be
a rest-over for the Greats:
Hank Williams, Kitty Wells,
The Carter Family
and Hank Snow.

It must be
because I've been told so,

because I know
two Metis women who sing
beyond the blue.

Tawow! Tawow!: Come in, you are welcome!

ODE TO THE GREATS (NORTHERN TRIBUTE)

Live

from the Grand Ole Opry
Hank cooed in all his glory

sailed

blue notes, fiddle strings
over airwaves,
pining lonesome,
his cheating heart
bursting through the voice box

up north

long before me, paved roads
and flushing toilets,

long before
the blues were reinvented,
sung
in a dozen shades of grey,
pale in comparison,

those rockabilly crooners
changed the soul
of heartland music

up north
before electric heat

they cuddled up to the woodstove,
toes tapping
along with Kitty, quivering
old-time twang,
her honky-tonk angels
bush and backroads
as Tennessee could never be,

crying blue
as Amigo's guitar
longing sweetly, strumming fingers
long past sundown

up north

a damn sight wild,
their generation,

half crazy on home brew
tuning hand-me-down guitars,
feet stomping
and lifting higher,
breaking into jigs
sweeping plywood floors

up north

long before power lines, oil rigs
burping underground

Patsy's syrup voice and sweet dreams
flowed from maple trees,
echoed far and wide
loons on the lake
crooning stars, pulling the moon

down
and through the voice box

Sara, A.P.
and Maybelle
picked autoharp strings,

chimed Clinch Mountain bluegrass
lonely
as muskeg reeds, spring frogs
pitching into chorus,
pining blue sky
orange, purple
crimson

up north

when the wind picks up,
blows sweet juniper
through the tent flaps,
the only thing to do
is sing, sing

strum and sing,
the northern lights
bright as Opryland,

dancing

the whole night through

they sang, their generation
sang
low and mean,
the poor man's blues,
richer than most

up north, before me,
before all roads
led down south

there was Heartland, USA

tuned in and

live

on the voice box
Jimmie and Wilf, all of
the Greats
chiming their Opry hi-dee-ho,
calling all lonesome rangers
to gather round

the voice box

up north

they sang and played
long after
the lights went down,

long after
the stage went silent,

the Greats
immortalized on records
that over time
skipped and scratched,

lifted me off to sleep

down south

my Greats, those two
homesick rounders
spoke of the north,
the glory days

as if it were only yesterday,
as if
one small ocean
could ever claim

their spirits, untamed,
sharp and tuned
as Hank's guitar.

Dorothy Scofield

was born in 1944 in Vancouver, British Columbia and grew up on a homestead in Whonnock, British Columbia. She lived in northern Saskatchewan, Manitoba and the Yukon, and she had a special affinity for the north. She loved literature and music and read everything from Edgar Cayce to the *Enquirer*. She wrote poetry and played the guitar and accordion, and she saw her all-time hero Wilf Carter in concert several times. She passed away in 1993.

Georgina Houle Young

was born in 1926 in Desmarias, Alberta and grew up in and around Wabasca, Alberta. She attended St. Martin's Convent School. She was married in 1946 and had three sons, all of whom passed away while still young. She came to British Columbia in the early 1970s after a long struggle with TB, met her common-law husband Harry and resettled in Maple Ridge. She was an avid beadworker, seamstress, storyteller and musician. She considered herself the "fourth" Carter Family member because she knew how to play and sing their every song. She passed away in 1996.

GREGORY SCOFIELD is a Metis poet, storyteller, activist and community worker of Cree, Scottish, English and French ancestry. He was born in British Columbia and raised in Saskatchewan, northern Manitoba and the Yukon. He has published three previous and highly praised books with Polestar Book Publishers: *The Gathering: Stones for the Medicine Wheel*; *Native Canadiana: Songs from the Urban Rez*; and *Love Medicine and One Song*. His autobiography is *Thunder Through My Veins: Memories of a Metis Childhood* (HarperCollins). Gregory Scofield lives in Maple Ridge, BC.

About Gregory Scofield's Previous Books:

The Gathering: Stones for the Medicine Wheel
In his first book of poetry, Scofield bridges Native and non-Native worlds, offering insight into the historical and contemporary displacement of Canada's Metis people.
WINNER OF THE DOROTHY LIVESAY POETRY PRIZE
0-919591-74-4 • $12.95 CAN / $10.95 USA • 96pp, pb
Now in its second printing.

Native Canadiana: Songs from the Urban Rez
These poems garnered Scofield the Canadian Authors Association Award for Most Promising Young Writer. "These poems … bring the gift and light and affirmation with a lyrical intensity that astonishes." — Patrick Lane
0-896095-12-7 • $14.95 CAN / $12.95 USA • 128 pp, pb
Now in its second printing.

Love Medicine and One Song
"…melds intensely erotic imagery with elements of the Canadian bush and the rhythm of Cree words and phrases … With an approach to writing that mingles tenderness with aggression, Scofield offers poems that come from an honest and candid place." — *See Magazine*
1-896095-27-5 • $16.95 CAN / $13.95 USA • 112 pp, pb

BRIGHT LIGHTS FROM POLESTAR

Polestar takes pride in creating books that enrich our understanding of the world, and in introducing discriminating readers to exciting writers. These independent voices illuminate our history, stretch the imagination and engage our sympathies.

POETRY:

Beatrice Chancy • *by George Elliott Clarke*
This brilliant dramatic poem is the first literary work to treat the issue of Canadian slavery. "Clarke … carries this story from our heads to our hearts to that gut feeling we all get when we have heard a devastating truth." — Nikki Giovanni
1-896095-94-1 • $16.95 CAN / $14.95 USA

Whylah Falls • *by George Elliott Clarke*
Clarke writes from the heart of Nova Scotia's Black community. Winner of the Archibald Lampman Award for poetry.
0-919591-57-4 • $14.95 CAN/$12.95 USA

Inward to the Bones: Georgia O'Keeffe's Journey with Emily Carr • *by Kate Braid*
In 1930, Emily Carr met Georgia O'Keeffe at an exhibition in New York. Inspired by this meeting, poet Kate Braid describes what might have happened afterwards.
1-896095-40-2 • $16.95 CAN/$13.95 USA

Blue Light in the Dash • *Brenda Brooks*
Like the best country ballad, these poems are pure eloquence; they sing about lesbian love and desire. By the author of *Somebody Should Kiss You*.
0-919591-99-X • $12.95 CAN/$10.95 USA

FICTION:

diss/ed banded nation • *by David Nandi Odhiambo*
"Thoroughly convincing in its evocation of young, rebellious, impoverished urban lives … an immersion into a simmering stew of racial and cultural identities…"
— *The Globe and Mail*
1-896095-26-7 • $16.95 CAN/$13.95 USA

Pool-Hopping and Other Stories • *by Anne Fleming*
Witty and engaging stories by a superb new writer. "Fleming's evenhanded, sharp-eyed and often hilarious narratives traverse the frenzied chaos of urban life with ease and precision." — *The Georgia Straight*
1-896095-18-6 • $16.95 CAN/$13.95 USA

West by Northwest: British Columbia Short Stories
edited by David Stouck and Myler Wilkinson
A brilliant collection of short fiction that celebrates the unique landscape and literary culture of BC. Includes stories by Bill Reid, Ethel Wilson, Emily Carr, Wayson Choy, George Bowering, Evelyn Lau, Shani Mootoo and others.
1-896095-41-0 • $18.95 CAN/$16.95 USA